MW01121181

Writing With Our Feet

DATE DUE

A PLAY

WRITING WITH OUR FEET

DAVE CARLEY

160201

Blizzard Publishing • Winnipeg

Writing With Our Feet first published 1992 by
Blizzard Publishing Inc.
301–89 Princess St., Winnipeg, Canada R3B 1K6
© 1990 Dave Carley

Cover design by Ryan Takatsu
Cover photo by Nir Bareket
Back cover photo by Michael Lee
Printed in Canada by Kromar Printing Ltd.

The photograph used for the cover is from the Factory Theatre
production of *Writing With Our Feet* and features (left) Tanya Jacobs
and Stephen Ouimette.

Published with the assistance of
the Canada Council and the Manitoba Arts Council.

Canadian Cataloguing in Publication Data
Carley, Dave, 1955-
  Writing with our feet
  A play.
  ISBN 0-921368-20-8
I. Title
PS8555.A7397W75 1992   C812/.54   C91-097173-0
PR9199.3.C274W75 1989

Dedication

My sister and I really did learn how to write with our feet. It was 1964 and the recent, unexpected death of a president was weighing heavily on our minds. If Kennedy could be bumped off so easily, what horrors awaited two youngsters living in Camelot's northernmost suburbs? At the very least: the loss of our hands. We were not impressed by our school insurance forms, which promised us a windfall $500 for each lopped-off extremity. We knew this wouldn't be enough. We knew we had to develop competent back-up systems. The entire neighbourhood could play at being outdoors children, but my sister and I huddled in the dark, practicing with our toes for an inevitable physiological Armageddon.

Nearly three decades have passed. Neither my sister nor I has yet to lose a body part. I'm beginning to think that footwriting in a darkened room while the rest of the world romps in the sun is some kind of metaphor.

Jean-Francois, my footwriting hero, eventually realizes his feet are best used for walking out in the world. My sister and I? We gave up footwriting and went into theatre. My sister found theatre first, but then again she was always a much better footwriter. This play is dedicated to her.

For Jan Carley

Writing With Our Feet was first produced as a one-act play—consisting of about the first twenty minutes of the full-length work—at Alberta Theatre Projects' playRites 90 Festival, in the Brief New Works showcase series. It was later given a staged reading by New York City's Theatre North Collective in March 1990, and then a full production by that same theatre in June 1990.

Writing With Our Feet, in its full-length form, was workshopped by Vancouver's Dark Horse Theatre in April 1990, and given a staged reading as part of the New Play Centre's SpringRites Festival. Participants in the workshop were Don Thompson and Nicole Robert. Robert Garfat, Artistic Director of Dark Horse, directed.

On October 12, 1990, the full-length version of *Writing With Our Feet* opened at Hamilton's Theatre Terra Nova, with the following cast:

JEAN-FRANCOIS   Nigel Hamer
SOPHIE, et al.   Suzanne Bélanger

Directed by Kevin Land
Set Design: Michael Adkins
Lighting Design: Christopher McHarge
Stage Manager: Barb Wright

I am indebted to a great number of individuals and institutions for their help with this script. Thanks first of all to Robert Garfat, who directed the Dark Horse Theatre workshop, and to its participants Nicole Robert and Don Thompson. I'm grateful also to Theatre Terra Nova's Chris McHarge and Kevin Land, and the original cast—Suzanne Bélanger and Nigel Hamer. Thanks also to Lesley Ewen, Jed Harris, Ellen Rae Hennessey, Tanja Jacobs, Ann Jansen, Annie Kidder, Jackie Maxwell, Patti Ney, Stephen Ouimette and Allan Zinyk. The help of the Canada Council, Carnegie Mellon Showcase of New Plays, Dark Horse Theatre, Department of External Affairs, Factory Theatre, Ontario Arts Council, Shaw Festival and Theatre Terra Nova is also gratefully acknowledged. Special thanks to Pierre Péloquin.

Characters

Jean-Francois
Sophie, Aunt Zénaïde, Alphonsinette, Lucy Cormier, Father Rocky,
Raymond Loewy

Non-traditional casting is encouraged.

Time

About now, or soon, and in the past, mostly after the death of Jean-Francois' parents and the recent death of his sister Sophie.

Place

A garage underneath an access ramp in Montreal.

Writing With Our Feet

(JEAN-FRANCOIS is in the garage, writing. He's wearing black. At the very least, he has pinned a black ribbon to his shirt or jacket.)

JEAN-FRANCOIS: Sophie and I were eight and ten when we began writing with our feet. Our tender minds had been deeply affected by the tragedy of our cousin Alphonsinette. After passing a long evening in disreputable company at the Arthabaska Hotel, she stretched herself across an abandoned rail-line and slid into deep sleep.

SOPHIE: *(Entering.)* Daddy's on the phone to Arthabaska! A rare train came and clipped off the legs of Alphonsinette!

JEAN-FRANCOIS: What!

SOPHIE: Her God-given legs! It's a one-in-a-million tragedy!

JEAN-FRANCOIS: Cousin Alph moved to Montréal and settled into the big wing-chair in the front room. She sat there and waited for her new legs to be made.

SOPHIE: Today's quote: "I drank to forget, now look what I've got to remember: a goddamn waist that ends in mid-air!"

(JEAN-FRANCOIS and SOPHIE laugh.)

JEAN-FRANCOIS: She crabbed for the three months it took a master carver from St. Jean-Port-Joli to do the legs. In the meantime, Maman dug up our old baby carriage and Papa cut off the sides and the canopy. So it'd look less like a pram and more like something you'd push an angry, legless twenty-three year old cousin in. The carriage worked so well, and Sophie and I were such obliging pilots, that when the wooden legs finally arrived, Alphonsinette rejected them on a technicality.

SOPHIE: *(Quoting.)* "I don't like the finish. And all this carving down the side! I'll look like a goddamn souvenir!"

JEAN-FRANCOIS: She said that?

SOPHIE: *(Quoting.)* "First Yank tourist to see me'll rip them off. My legs'll end up on some mantelpiece in Pittsburgh! Send them back!"

JEAN-FRANCOIS: Daddy must be berserk!

SOPHIE: *(Quoting.)* "She's lazy! I'm showing her the golden toe!"

JEAN-FRANCOIS: And Papa did indeed give Alphonsinette the boot, forcing the government to assume her care. They bought her a wheel-chair with a converted Evinrude and today, decades later, she's a familiar sight along rue St. Laurent, buzzing from bar to bar, sounding like a thirsty fishing boat.

SOPHIE: We can learn from this, Jean-Francois.

JEAN-FRANCOIS: How?

SOPHIE: Alphie lost her legs to teach us the big lesson.

JEAN-FRANCOIS: Sophie believed that horrible events occurred to warn the as-yet-unscathed. Even at eight my sister was on the cutting edge of a dark theology.

SOPHIE: Look at her! Angry! A pillow of a woman! She zigzags along St. Laurent like a drunken waterbeetle. Trying to forget what's van-ished. Completely unprepared for life's vagaries!

JEAN-FRANCOIS: What's your point?

SOPHIE: What if we lost a limb or two? What if we lost our hands? We can't lose our legs because of the law of averages, not when two legs are already missing from the family tree.

(JEAN-FRANCOIS and SOPHIE regard their hands.)

But these—the innocent hands of the child.

JEAN-FRANCOIS: Fodder for fate.

SOPHIE: Can you imagine the horror?

JEAN-FRANCOIS: But how!

SOPHIE: Not a train—that family law of averages is against it. But a bloody encounter with an overturned lawn-mower during a three-legged race! That'd do it!

JEAN-FRANCOIS: Or Papa, deranged by drink, attacking us with a machete as we sleep with arms upraised.

SOPHIE: Oh J-F, we've got to get competent back-up systems! What if Alphonsinette had taught herself to walk with her hands? At the very worst she could be doing bar-counter handstands for drink money! As for you and me … we'll learn to write—with our feet!

(JEAN-FRANCOIS and SOPHIE regard their feet.)

JEAN-FRANCOIS: Recognizing the wisdom of my sister's words, we set out on a program of foot-training, showing such determination that the story of Sophie and myself is, in effect, the history of footwriting in the Americas—

SOPHIE: I'm going to use a typewriter—

JEAN-FRANCOIS: And this garage, this was our stage—

SOPHIE: God may take away our hands but surely He'll leave us electricity.

JEAN-FRANCOIS: In no time at all Sophie was up to twenty words a minute.

SOPHIE: Shit! My big toe just hit four keys at once. I was going for the L and I wrote PLOK!

JEAN-FRANCOIS: Eventually even the big toe hurdle was leapt, and Sophie could, with the daintiest of twitches, hit just one key at a time. Me, I let her use the typewriter and I worked up a kind of longhand. I'd hold my pen, which I wrapped with hockey tape for stickiness, between the big toe and toe two, and off I'd go.

Our pre-teen years passed. Then our teens. Then our post-teens. Sophie got faster and faster. She could pound out a letter to our Aunt Zénaïde in Arthabaska, a three-pager, in less than fifteen minutes. She even learned to fold the paper and stuff it into a foot-addressed envelope. For my part, I developed a languid script; large, because footwriting is not so economical of paper, but very lovely, a source of admiration to us both.

SOPHIE: It's artistic, Jean-Francois! You've got real style! That's a gentleman's hand you've got in that foot!

JEAN-FRANCOIS: Eventually a new dilemma presented itself, as dilemmas always do.

SOPHIE: *(Groans.)* Where does this lead? I can't spend the rest of my life writing letters to Arthabaskan aunties!

JEAN-FRANCOIS: I don't see why not!

SOPHIE: Granted, our inheritance means we don't have to work. And this garage is comfy—who can knock a life of footwriting in the shadow of this Willys Aero Ace? But surely there's more to reach for in life.

JEAN-FRANCOIS: Like what?

SOPHIE: I don't know. Philosophies.

JEAN-FRANCOIS: *(Understanding.)* Ah—philosophies.

SOPHIE: I'm going to write instructional motifs with my feet. It's a different genre than Auntie letters and, though I've no wish to diminish letter-writing, this *is* tougher. Especially when one must project the muse through one's toes.

JEAN-FRANCOIS: I have to tell you the major difference between Sophie and me. Yes, we were related by blood and, yes, we shared many fears and aspirations. But nevertheless, there was a fundamental dissimilarity in our brains. *(Pause.)* I'm a generalist. I see the big picture. Vaguely, imprecisely, but I've got the whole ball of wax in my viewfinder. With Sophie everything got narrowed to one precise point of accessible wisdom, and she'd see that point with perfect clarity. A reductivist Kahlil Gibran.

SOPHIE: I have to repeat a word.

JEAN-FRANCOIS: Myself, I'd repeat hundreds of them, sometimes for no other reason than I enjoyed their peculiar combinations of letters. I'd scrawl them out, add adjectives, adverbs, contractions...

SOPHIE: I hate like hell repeating a word when I'm only using thirteen of them in the first place—but when I read this you'll see the necessity, I hope.

(SOPHIE types.)

JEAN-FRANCOIS: It embarrasses me to read my early work. Once, during an argument over something else—

SOPHIE: You're the reincarnation of Alfred, Lord Tennyson! *(Pause.)* I'm sorry, I'm sorry, I take it back.

JEAN-FRANCOIS: No—you're right.

SOPHIE: Tennyson was too strong. Uh—Sir Walter Scott.

JEAN-FRANCOIS: That's worse! Soph, why don't you just say it? I'm bombastic and florid!

SOPHIE: People can't cope with bulk. They don't have the attention span. And you have to have endings!

JEAN-FRANCOIS: I could never finish a thought—but I could always add another stanza. You see, if I finished something I'd have to let it be judged. That was scary, so I'd go and tackle giant historical movements and stay at them for a year or more—the populist wit of Adlai Stevenson, the design eloquence of Raymond Loewy. Well, why not! I'd flex the toes and that'd be it, page after page after page—

SOPHIE: Almost done!

JEAN-FRANCOIS: But hers: anorexic jottings, environmentally correct in their careful use of space and paper ... politically correct in their preoccupation with the big themes of our century. Sophie began just after the New Deal, mostly because that's when Papa's collection of *Life* magazines started. She'd reached the Sixties by the time she died.

SOPHIE: Okay! You want to hear it? *(Performs.)* I'm dedicating this one to my cousin Terry, the owner of this car, a man who understands exile and the enduring hatred of Family.

JEAN-FRANCOIS: *(Catching her in time.)* Funding bodies!

SOPHIE: Oh! My thanks to the *ministère des affaires culturelles*, and to the estate of my parents. Instruction 343.

"Medgar Evers
Walking walking
Moon shining
Gun glinting
America's dreaming
Chews Mississippi asphalt."

(Pause.) So?

JEAN-FRANCOIS: I like it.

SOPHIE: What about "chews"?

JEAN-FRANCOIS: Bites?

SOPHIE: I thought of that, but I want the image of his face grinding into pavement.

JEAN-FRANCOIS: It's sad.

SOPHIE: And life is happy?

JEAN-FRANCOIS: It's a long poem, for you.

SOPHIE: I measured it. There's a hand-dryer above the sinks and I can fit it right on the side. *(Packing up.)* It's perfect.

(SOPHIE has Scotch tape, paper.)

JEAN-FRANCOIS: My sister, she's dead now, she's just—gone now—that's another story and one that makes less sense than anything else I could tell you. It always falls to the living to create meaning out of what's gone before.... For me it's always come from Sophie the Reductivist, out here in this garage, from her feet....

(SOPHIE kisses JEAN-FRANCOIS on the cheek.)

SOPHIE: *(Exiting.)* I'll be back in an hour. I'll pick up a pizza on the way home.

(SOPHIE exits.)

JEAN-FRANCOIS: She'd finish a work, shoot out of the garage and off our property. She scattered her writings about the city, pinning them to trees, taping them to stop signs.... Her most famous ones were the God/Agog series. The entire message was God/Agog, but there were variations: God/Gagged. God/Gone. Good/God. She pasted these to churches and the *Gazette* ran a picture once of a sexton scraping God/Agog off the front door of Christ Church Cathedral.

Mostly she worked at the bus and plane terminals. She knew that was where her words had their greatest effect, their maximum exposure, short of publication, which she opposed on environmental grounds. People would come to the bus terminal, or Dorval; they'd see her motifs and, because they were so brief, they'd carry them in their minds to wherever they were headed—to every corner of the province or any city of the world.

You see, we're really just two stops from anyplace else. Dorval to Djakarta, Djakarta to Kupang, Kupang to Dili. Two stopovers. All the way to Timor and such a small chain along which to pass the equally concise thought. The world can be a giant thought-chain—and it was *my* sister who discovered this.

Sophie's work—her last was the one she just did on Medgar Evers—it's all still circling about, taped from wall to wall, moving from terminal to terminal, but most often just passing from mind to mind. Tiny potent foot creations. Circling the planet. Sophie's reductivist ideology, everywhere.

This, then, is the comfort I derive. My sister has died without losing the use of her hands. You can over-prepare. Me, I still sit here and write with my feet because, Sophie having escaped that fate, the odds are higher now I'll lose mine. And I'm shortening up. As soon as I get down to a manageable length I'll rejuvenate that chain of words my sister began. I'll leave here. I will. *(Unconvinced.)* Of course I will.

And—oh yes—to return to where it all started: Cousin Alphonsinette. She's met a lusty boy from Arvida who says her legs would only have been in the way. That seems to make her happy on some level. They live above Le Vagabond Hotel and I'm told they've even found a priest who's willing to marry them. Which proves there's salvation for us all, even if we haven't spent a lifetime preparing for the worst.

·

The Compassion of Aunt Zénaïde

(AUNT ZÉNAÏDE bursts into the garage, wearing black.)

AUNT ZÉNAÏDE: *(Off.)* Allo allo!

JEAN-FRANCOIS: *(To himself.)* Aunt Zénaïde.

AUNT ZÉNAÏDE: *(Bursting on.)* My boy, my boy, my boy! My poor benighted boy! *(etc.)*

> *(AUNT ZÉNAÏDE kisses and hugs JEAN-FRANCOIS and squeezes him to her ample bosom.)*

JEAN-FRANCOIS: And then there's the relatives....

AUNT ZÉNAÏDE: The agony you must be feeling!

JEAN-FRANCOIS: Cousins and uncles and demented aunts.

AUNT ZÉNAÏDE: Poor, poor Jean-Francois! An orphan! A brand-new orphan....

JEAN-FRANCOIS: The oppression of blood and bosom ...

AUNT ZÉNAÏDE: How can you hold up? How can you carry on? What prevents you from smashing your brains out in grief? When a baby dies it takes a mother's arms six months to recover, to stop feeling the ache for holding her child. How long will it take you to get over losing your Maman and Papa!

JEAN-FRANCOIS: For another year my ass will feel echoes of the belt!

AUNT ZÉNAÏDE: *(Decks him.)* Don't speak bad of the recently dead!

JEAN-FRANCOIS: It's the truth!

> *(AUNT ZÉNAÏDE decks him again.)*

AUNT ZÉNAÏDE: I don't care! Beating is our heritage! *(Pressing JEAN-FRANCOIS back against her.)* Your Papa beat you, he beat Sophie, Xenon beats me, we all beat each other. It's the family glue.

JEAN-FRANCOIS: Where's Sophie?

AUNT ZÉNAÏDE: She ran out of the house.

JEAN-FRANCOIS: Is she OK?

AUNT ZÉNAÏDE: How could she be, with her parents mouldering.

JEAN-FRANCOIS: Did she have Scotch tape on her?

AUNT ZÉNAÏDE: As a matter of fact, yes, she did.

JEAN-FRANCOIS: She's at the bus terminal.

AUNT ZÉNAÏDE: I wish you could've come.

JEAN-FRANCOIS: I've already explained why.

AUNT ZÉNAÏDE: And it's a perfectly good explanation. I'm not like all the other asswipe relatives. They never had a minute for your poor parents and now they turn around and say, "Where's Jean-Francois? What an ungrateful child not to see his own folks into the ground!" Those Pharisees. But couldn't you have sat outside in the long black car?

JEAN-FRANCOIS: No.

AUNT ZÉNAÏDE: Of course you couldn't. *(Gathers him in again.)* It was a beautiful service. Apart from the religious stuff. The priest is a dolt. The homily was on dead birds. I tell you, they should bring back the Latin. That way you can only suspect what a pack of morons they all are. Dead birds! *(Pause.)* By the way, what does God/Agog mean?

JEAN-FRANCOIS: It's an instruction.

AUNT ZÉNAÏDE: To who?

JEAN-FRANCOIS: To you, for starters.

AUNT ZÉNAÏDE: *(Decks him.)* I don't like your tone! Anyway, if it's an instruction, it's a piss-poor one.

JEAN-FRANCOIS: Why do you ask?

AUNT ZÉNAÏDE: I went up for communion and when I returned your poor sister had taped it to the back of the pew.

JEAN-FRANCOIS: Did Sophie go up for communion?

AUNT ZÉNAÏDE: No, she sat there like a stoic and when it was over she ran out and didn't say a word to any of the family. I don't blame her. Alphonsinette was drunk, of course. She had a flask on her and now she's back at Le Vagabond, getting pie-faced with that wastrel husband of mine. Well, I'm giving Xenon another hour, then I'm pulling him out of there by the hairy ear. The car needs gassing. We won't stay over. I can't sleep unless I'm in my Arthabaska bed. *(She smothers*

JEAN-FRANCOIS again.) You poor thing. You're not equipped for life. *(Cunning pause.)* Was there an estate?

JEAN-FRANCOIS: Mmmnnnppph …

AUNT ZÉNAÏDE: A big one, a small one, in-between one …

JEAN-FRANCOIS: Mmmnnnppph …

AUNT ZÉNAÏDE: I suppose your mother brought something to the marriage but my brother was as useless as tits on a brass monkey.

JEAN-FRANCOIS: Mmmnnnppph …

AUNT ZÉNAÏDE: Sophie can go out and work. She types such beautiful letters to me, she could go work for a solicitor, maybe even an English one.

JEAN-FRANCOIS: *(Coming up for air.)* We'll be fine.

AUNT ZÉNAÏDE: So there is money!

JEAN-FRANCOIS: Enough.

AUNT ZÉNAÏDE: I'm so—relieved. For you. You could move to Arthabaska and live with us. I'll only offer once. You remember our house. We could fix up the garage just like this and even move that Willys Aero Ace back with you. Why you've kept it all these years is an incomprehension. Why that ass Terry bought it in the first place— I don't know the answer to that, either. In 1955 they built just six thousand of these and any fool would have known from that the car was going the way of the dodo. Everyone else buys a Chev in 1955 except our Terry—no, he has to be different. And that's not the only way he varied from the norm—

JEAN-FRANCOIS: We'll stay here.

AUNT ZÉNAÏDE: I won't offer twice.

JEAN-FRANCOIS: Thanks anyway.

AUNT ZÉNAÏDE: It's your choice. I could use the company. All I do in Arthabaska anymore is sit and think. Xenon doesn't talk much and when he does say something it isn't worth hearing. You and Sophie are educated … but if you won't come you won't come. I'm not like the rest of the family, I don't belabour a point. Ah, your Daddy—he was a good man. Don't ever forget that. Sure he had a temper, but that's genetic. Nothing you can do about genetics.

But to die the way your folks died, ah, it tears out my heart. I don't give two hoots about your Maman, she made him move here and I can't forgive her that. My favourite brother forced to move to Montréal, where he's a stinking fish out of water. And I curse Bombardier. I curse the day the first skidoo rolled off the assembly line. That they should all die in such a collective manner. Ten skidoos. Ten couples. All plunging simultaneously through the ice of Lac Aylmer. And not one of the wives sitting behind her stinking husband. Because they were swapping, eh.

(JEAN-FRANCOIS groans.)

You knew they were swapping.

JEAN-FRANCOIS: Yes, yes—

AUNT ZÉNAÏDE: The Philistine relatives talked of nothing else, all through the holy service. No doubt the swapping was the idea of your Maman. Urban slut. And for them to get fished out of Lac Aylmer after a week. Twenty corpses frozen like human ice-cubes. And for them to be shoved into those cheap plywood coffins because the funeral home ran out of good ones.

(JEAN-FRANCOIS is getting radically bugged.)

And then to be driving back to Montréal and have the hearse hit that propane truck. And both vehicles blow sky high. And then to discover that just before the accident the back door of the hearse had fallen open. And your boxed parents had shot out and landed in a frozen ditch. Where they skidded through the dead bulrushes. And, unlike Moses, no Pharaoh's daughter happens along to save them.

(JEAN-FRANCOIS is about to burst.)

Oh no, it has to be a pack of hungry, thrill-seeking dogs!

JEAN-FRANCOIS: Would you shut your fucking mouth!

AUNT ZÉNAÏDE: I'm so glad to hear you say that! Already you're getting your spark back and your parents aren't even in the ground! They hadn't dug the hole yet—had I told you that? Because of the strike. So we had to leave your Maman and Papa lying there—*(Holds nose.)* Phew—

JEAN-FRANCOIS: I'll hit you into next week!

AUNT ZÉNAÏDE: Spoken like your Papa! This is a good sign! *(Opens her bag.)* Now. I've got some things for you. I've got to yank that bastard Xenon out of Le Vagabond but first: Canada's Food Guide. Follow it. The army's 5BX Plan. Do it. You need some muscles but don't get like that pervert Terry. There are muscles and then there are "muscles". Terry's are "muscles". Here: this is a history of Laurier. Read it. He was from Arthabaska, sort of, and this will show you how far you can go in life. Remember: it was Jean Lesage upon whose knee you dandled.

JEAN-FRANCOIS: I remember that!

AUNT ZÉNAÏDE: *(Decks him.)* You were one and a half! Anyway, there's a passage in here about Lesage dandling off Laurier's knee. I've marked the page. Who can say where Laurier himself dandled? But there's a definite line of succession forming.

Finally: television. I've made a list of all the uplifting shows on TV. It's OK to give up on God but, if you do, you should watch more CBC. And nature shows. Watch those nature shows. "Turtles of Costa Rica." That kind of thing. That's as good as anything a priest can tell you.

JEAN-FRANCOIS: I hate turtle shows!

AUNT ZÉNAÏDE: Of course you do.

JEAN-FRANCOIS: They make me suicidal.

AUNT ZÉNAÏDE: That's the whole point! You look over the edge once or twice, you don't feel so bad you're up to your waist in shit.

JEAN-FRANCOIS: The plot's always the same. A mother turtle scrapes across a beach and lays a thousand eggs. Cute baby turtles hatch and with a sense of urgency crawl back towards water. But the sky starts swarming with vultures, swooping, snatching. And from the jungle, other animals emerge. Turtle-munchers. I'm to watch this in my tender state?

AUNT ZÉNAÏDE: But one of them always makes it to water!

JEAN-FRANCOIS: One out of a thousand! And you can bet your sweet life it's the one turtle with a totally retrograde personality, the real scumsucker—

AUNT ZÉNAÏDE: No! Can't you see—the one who makes it is the noble one! The Jean Lesage turtle! The Adlai Stevenson turtle!

(Crash offstage.)

JEAN-FRANCOIS: What's that?

AUNT ZÉNAÏDE: Sounds like that bastard Xenon! Hunting for booze in the kitchen of the recently dead. No pride on that one. I have to go. I'm glad we had this talk. I understand you better. *(At door.)* I know you don't believe and neither do I, but just to cover the bases: God bless you Jean-Francois! May He grant you peace and serenity and all that.

(AUNT ZÉNAÏDE exits. Immediately offstage hollering at Uncle Xenon, going under JEAN-FRANCOIS' next speech.)

You drunken bastard! You scumsucking turtlefucker! Get out of that booze! Take that! Take that! And that!

(More roaring offstage. JEAN-FRANCOIS may look in at them, shake head, return, talk.)

JEAN-FRANCOIS: The battle was joined. Aunt Zénaïde versus that sad excuse of a man Xenon. After a while Sophie came home and laid into them both. My parents were barely dead and not even properly buried and already my kitchen was a battlefield.

But perhaps I had been touched by Lesage and maybe some kind of inspiration had in fact passed to me because that night I wrote the only phrases of my florid youth that had any value ... while Sophie lay in her bed sobbing, I wrote poems that told of my isolation and my desire to escape ... long, silent yearnings from the heart, via the foot, that sang of who I was and what I might become, if only I could begin to dream. If only I could see what was at the centre of the ball of wax. If only I could pounce on the necessary system of thought. I was trying to give up on God, yes, but nobody in his right mind gives up a guardian angel or two ... Jean, Adlai, Raymond Loewy ... better them on your shoulder than turtle vultures above your head....

Sophie? Sophie?

(JEAN-FRANCOIS goes to the door, looks into the house, comes to.)

Oh Jesus, of course ... I forgot ... I hear a noise, I still think it's Sophie coming home.... I'd listen for her to come home from Dorval or wherever she was taping up her work....

They say a mother's arms can ache ... well, so can a brother's heart. Yeah, it can really ache.

The Visitation of Raymond Loewy

(Including JEAN-FRANCOIS, SOPHIE and RAYMOND LOEWY.)

JEAN-FRANCOIS: Sophie? Sophie....

(SOPHIE is at the door.)

SOPHIE: They've gone. I just waved them off.

JEAN-FRANCOIS: About time.

SOPHIE: Xenon's drunk but he's still got to drive, naturally. Aunt Zed insists they've had no problems since they chucked the St. Christopher's medal. But when Xenon backed over the Cormiers' lawn—I saw her crossing herself.

JEAN-FRANCOIS: How was the funeral?

SOPHIE: About what you'd expect. It's over, that's the best I can say.

JEAN-FRANCOIS: Aunt Zénaïde said they were all there.

SOPHIE: It was a circus. Lots of gossip. A chorus of clucking tongues. *(Leaving.)* Lucy Cormier says "hi" and Aphonsinette sends her "profuse love". Father Rocky is threatening to visit and there's a rumour Cousin Terry's heading east in a Nash Metropolitan.

JEAN-FRANCOIS: You're kidding!

SOPHIE: It's just a rumour. *(At the door.)* Did you have any supper?

JEAN-FRANCOIS: I wasn't hungry. Can't you stay?

SOPHIE: No. Not now. I need to be alone.

JEAN-FRANCOIS: There's beer in the fridge—

SOPHIE: Xenon stole it all. I'm going to my room.

JEAN-FRANCOIS: Soph?

(SOPHIE has left.)

Sophie. Sophie!

(SOPHIE turns, comes back into the light. She is RAYMOND LOEWY now.)

RAYMOND LOEWY: Sophie? How in Hades do I resemble your sister?

(RAYMOND LOEWY walks into the light.)

JEAN-FRANCOIS: *(Under breath.)* Raymond—Loewy?

RAYMOND LOEWY: I expected a different reception. A tentative hosanna—

JEAN-FRANCOIS: It *is* you! My God!

RAYMOND LOEWY: That's a bit excessive. I'd settle for a dim smile of recognition.

JEAN-FRANCOIS: Mr. Loewy! Mr. Loewy, sir!

RAYMOND LOEWY: Too effusive! You're sounding like one of my junior designers. Find a balance.

(Warm continental greeting.)

Raymond to you. Always, Raymond.

JEAN-FRANCOIS: I've wanted to meet you ever since, since I first held one of your Coke bottles, since I lit my first—

RAYMOND LOEWY: *(Offering.)* Cigarette?

JEAN-FRANCOIS: Luckies?

RAYMOND LOEWY: Just the packet. I fill it with Sobranies now, but I keep my packet, for appearances. It's not the end of the world if appearances deceive. Particularly with cigarettes.

JEAN-FRANCOIS: And it's a beautiful packet.

(RAYMOND LOEWY clears throat disapprovingly.)

RAYMOND LOEWY: "Beautiful"?

JEAN-FRANCOIS: Effective?

RAYMOND LOEWY: That's a bit better.

JEAN-FRANCOIS: Essential form reduced to elegance.

(RAYMOND LOEWY lights JEAN-FRANCOIS' cigarette and his. JEAN-FRANCOIS draws on his cigarette. RAYMOND LOEWY watches carefully.)

RAYMOND LOEWY: No, no! Smoke it like this! *(Exhales continentally.)* You're holding on to it like you're from Pittsburgh! And when you stand, turn your right foot out a bit. Pose.

JEAN-FRANCOIS: We're in my garage!

RAYMOND LOEWY: Personal design transcends interiors. That might be wise. Write it down, later. And not with your foot. I can no longer ignore this.

JEAN-FRANCOIS: It's a Willys Aero Ace.

RAYMOND LOEWY: I know. 1955. What's it doing here?

JEAN-FRANCOIS: It's my cousin Terry's.

RAYMOND LOEWY: It's a monstrosity.

JEAN-FRANCOIS: *(Starting to imitate RAYMOND LOEWY, with intermittent success.)* So's Terry. He had to flee the province, and he ditched the car with us. He lives in Hollywood now.

RAYMOND LOEWY: Are you wondering why I'm here?

JEAN-FRANCOIS: A little, yes.

RAYMOND LOEWY: I sensed you were in trouble. That you were floundering.

> *(JEAN-FRANCOIS starts to disagree.)*

My son, may I ask you a question? With whom do you speak in the course of the long, long day?

JEAN-FRANCOIS: Hardly anybody.

RAYMOND LOEWY: I was afraid of that.

JEAN-FRANCOIS: Just Aunt Zénaïde and Uncle Xenon. They phone. And Madame Cormier from across the street looks in, though I try to discourage her. The Korean sends his son around with the groceries. People knock on my door selling causes—

RAYMOND LOEWY: I have some advice for you. But first, an historical rationale. I am Parisian by birth. I came to America when I was twenty-six—

JEAN-FRANCOIS: —I know. You had a quarter in your pocket when you came and by the time you'd died you had houses in Manhattan, on the Riviera—

RAYMOND LOEWY: When I arrived here I was still young enough that I could graft new world vigour to my aesthetic preconceptions. *(Grimacing.)* Oh, that Aero Ace. It was style suicide. I warned them! "It's half Ford, half Hudson!" You can meld influences and achieve beauty but you can also end up wallowing in a slough of inconsequence. It's a common enough crime. Some entire nations do it.

JEAN-FRANCOIS: That's not fair!

RAYMOND LOEWY: Pardon?

JEAN-FRANCOIS: Sir.

RAYMOND LOEWY: I'm thinking of Belgium. Aren't you?

JEAN-FRANCOIS: Oh. Yeah. Yeah, Belgium's pretty dismal.

RAYMOND LOEWY: This cousin Terry—is he in the movies?

JEAN-FRANCOIS: Parts of him.

RAYMOND LOEWY: That explains so much.

(Car horn.)

That's Mrs. Loewy, she's tired and fractious. I'm worried about you. *(Leaving; turns.)* I'm a man of infinite ego, so I can only say this once. You are my last disciple. You alone on this woebegone continent have kept the faith. My work has been bastardized beyond redemption. My bulletnose cars are centrepieces in fern bars. There's graffiti in the lobby of the Lever Building. My Brazilian city is covered by the soot of a dying Amazon. I am dead! I can't fight back by creating anymore. There are no more Studebakers in my future, no more non-rusting refrigerator shelves....

(Car horn; impatient.)

You have always loved my work and you've devoted part of your life to its study. I'm honoured. But even the best-read disciple must go forth and spread the gospel sooner or later, don't you think?

(JEAN-FRANCOIS looks away.)

There is something inside you, struggling to—emerge ...

(Car horn; insistent.)

And there is something else wanting to kill it. Who will win this little donnybrook?

(Horn.)

This is no good. That woman will wake the dead. We'll stop by on our way back.

(Leaving; turns; throws Lucky Strike pack.)

Goodbye my Jean-Francois. Smoke in style, heh?

(RAYMOND LOEWY exits.)

A Man's Home

(With JEAN-FRANCOIS and an offstage SOPHIE.)

JEAN-FRANCOIS: "Something in me—struggling to emerge." Emerge emerge emerge. Emerge from where? Nobody has any respect for the garage academic. *(Chomping about.)* What about study? What about the ivory tower? Ivory—garage. *(Stops; this might be worth writing down; goes to chair.)* See, I just thought of that. *(Writing with foot.)* "The Ivory Garage." A poem by—a longish poem by Jean-Francois. *(Writes.)* As the lemming flees to the sea. *(Correction.)* Hotfoots to sea. *(Mumbling.)* No, it's cold up there. Coldfoots. Hiphops. Snowshoes. *(Thinking about writing.)* All change is like an iceberg. All thought is like an iceberg. So very much submerged. Emerged. Ack. Submerged. Only one-tenth … a ninth? A ninth or tenth—Only a portion glints in the cold sunlight and … and … *(Crumples up sheet, quietly.)* Fuck.

(Picks up hub-cap.)

Well, my little foundling, we're having another uninspired day. When the access ramp was built over our gully *(Nods in its direction.)* it wasn't one day before these things began raining down on our house! Maman was having her beer in the deck chair and she nearly got beaned by the first, a Pontiac. Cool as a cucumber, she turns it over *(Continentally.)*— et voila: ashtray.

But the hub-caps—they land on the roof and skid off our eaves; they bang on to here and saucer out onto the street. Sophie used to run out and grab them before the Cormiers did—Madame Cormier's a collector, too. It wasn't long before we had all the ashtrays we needed—one for every table and chair arm—so now I hang them here.

The last time I was out the front door, all the way out, I was chasing a Plymouth. I heard it rolling across the roof and I could see the witch Cormier throwing on her coat, so I ran out fast. I didn't even think about being outside; I certainly didn't think about propping the door open.

I chased it down the street—only three houses, but I was out of breath—I hadn't started the 5BX at this point—Cormier's hot on my heels but I get there first, I grab it and then I remember how far away I am. I look back—big mistake—and there's the house and the garage, it's like they're on another planet. I'd never really seen how this place huddled under the access ramp....

I'm nauseous, faint ... a white roar is jamming my skull. I walk, one foot in front of the other, not running, just walking, trying to be calm, past the Martins', then the Rhéaumes', then Monsieur Péloquin's, then across our lawn, up the stoop and just as I reach my front door *(Makes noise.)*—it blows shut.

I smash at it with my shoulder but it's stubborn, it won't give way. "You're doomed!" Madame Cormier is crowing, rejoicing in my terror. There's one basement window and I kick at it. I kick out the divider strip and some of the glass and then I dive through. I hurl myself through—glass gouges at my back and my shoulders, it rips my scalp in long, vicious licks ... but I'm inside. I'm inside, again. Safe.

Cormier peered in at me. She had the hub-cap. She wouldn't go away until I swore at her.

SOPHIE: *(Offstage; warning.)* Alphonsinette!

JEAN-FRANCOIS: Huh? *(Back to story.)* That was the last time I was out. If I ever see another hub-cap rolling down my street I'll remind myself I've got enough. Cormier can help herself.

SOPHIE: *(Offstage; warning.)* Alphonsinette!

JEAN-FRANCOIS: Christ, Alphonsinette. *(Back to story.)* This is a roundabout way of telling you there aren't many advantages to living in the shade of an access ramp. No one even knows what it's giving access to! It's the same one Cousin Terry escaped on—maybe it leads to Hollywood. *(Shrugs continentally.)*

SOPHIE: *(Offstage.)* Alphonsinette's coming!

(Growing sound of Evinrude outboard.)

JEAN-FRANCOIS: *(Pulling paper up; footwriting.)* "Concerning hub-cap avarice: Propelled by it, he took many risks, many times leaving his flanks exposed—"

SOPHIE: *(Offstage.)* She's at the driveway! I'm hiding!

JEAN-FRANCOIS: "—but his passion for dulling chrome, the flotsam of accessing vehicles, blinded him to the tearing hunks of his soul."

Alphonsinette's Brilliant Scheme

(ALPHONSINETTE roars into the garage on her motorized wheel-chair. It should have an Evinrude outboard mounted on the back for propulsion, and maybe a Studebaker bulletnose.)

ALPHONSINETTE: Great stuff, Jean-Francois! Powerful! It's a strong argument for feet! God, were you smart to stay away from that funeral! Where's your sister?

JEAN-FRANCOIS: Probably downtown.

ALPHONSINETTE: She's always downtown!

JEAN-FRANCOIS: Well, that's where she is. *(Tries to resume work.)* You could try the bus terminal.

ALPHONSINETTE: Come on! This is no time to be anti-social! How often do I visit? How often do your parents have a funeral, for that matter? I'm family. Don't turn your back on family. After all, who can defend you from family, but family? And listen, I would have come yesterday but I had to wait until that maniac Xenon was gone. *(Pause.)* And I'm truly sorry.

JEAN-FRANCOIS: Thanks.

ALPHONSINETTE: It makes no difference to me they were Swappers. I feel their loss just as keenly. After I lost my legs, things didn't look so bright for old Alphonsinette. Maybe a job in a circus, maybe a lecture tour of the CEGEPs, warning of the perils of drink. But your Papa, my good uncle, he took me in.

JEAN-FRANCOIS: He also kicked you out.

ALPHONSINETTE: That was my fault and I bear him no malice. I'll never forget that before he kicked me out, he took me in.

JEAN-FRANCOIS: We had a good time pushing you up and down the street.

ALPHONSINETTE: And the way you'd hurtle me around the corner on two wheels. Ah, those were the days. *(Cunning pause.)* Yes, those days remain a beacon of happiness to me amid the dimming light of my life.

JEAN-FRANCOIS: How're things at the hotel?

ALPHONSINETTE: Fine. Wonderful. Except they're tearing it down.

JEAN-FRANCOIS: Ahh—

ALPHONSINETTE: It's historical.

JEAN-FRANCOIS: I see.

ALPHONSINETTE: It might remind people of things if you were to leave it standing there. People approach memories in the strangest ways. Especially politicians.

(Banging noise.)

What the hell's that?

JEAN-FRANCOIS: Probably a hub-cap. *(Gets up and peeks out.)* There it goes off the curb. Cormier's already in hot pursuit—she's got a sixth sense for them now.

ALPHONSINETTE: *(Looking.)* She can really move for an old cotton top.

JEAN-FRANCOIS: It's turning the corner, it'll be at the Korean's—

ALPHONSINETTE: *(Feigning interest.)* Ah yeah, there it goes ... I was wondering—

JEAN-FRANCOIS: Sophie and I are happy here, together. Thank you for offering to move in with us.

(ALPHONSINETTE protests.)

Whenever anyone praises my writing I know they're heading for a big request and when you told me about your hotel ... We want to live alone. Anyway, I thought you had a boyfriend from Arvida!

ALPHONSINETTE: I do!

JEAN-FRANCOIS: Tell him to put you up!

ALPHONSINETTE: I thought he could move here, too. You'd like him. You're very similar. You're stuck in here and Arvida, well, he won't come out of the bedroom. Things don't look so good for us once they tear down Le Vagabond. The city's expensive now and we've only got little pensions.

JEAN-FRANCOIS: Big enough for beer.

ALPHONSINETTE: But not enough to—ah—set us up in business.

JEAN-FRANCOIS: What qualifies you for business?

ALPHONSINETTE: Initiative. Foresight. Creativity. Plus an idea. Hold up your finger. Come on. Give me your thumb.

> *(JEAN-FRANCOIS does. ALPHONSINETTE sprays something on it from a small, mouth spray-like container, with an air of intense concentration.)*

JEAN-FRANCOIS: What're you doing? What is this? It's turning to rubber!

ALPHONSINETTE: It's the idea of the century!

JEAN-FRANCOIS: What is it?

ALPHONSINETTE: Spray-on condoms!

JEAN-FRANCOIS: What?

ALPHONSINETTE: Think about it! What's the biggest problem facing us today? Everyone hates using condoms. We know we're supposed to—we know we have to—but even the most inventive lover has difficulty installing the latex condom without calling for a minor intermission.... And they don't feel right.

JEAN-FRANCOIS: How do you know?

ALPHONSINETTE: My man says it's like shaking hands with a skidoo mitt over your wiener.

> *(JEAN-FRANCOIS is laughing.)*

Come on, JF, hear me out! Answer me this: what does the modern person do best?

JEAN-FRANCOIS: Watch TV.

ALPHONSINETTE: *(Slugs him.)* Spray, dummy! Spray!

JEAN-FRANCOIS: —Spray, spray.

ALPHONSINETTE: We spend our lives spraying ovens, lawns, hair.... So picture the scene, JF. A couple in the final throes of foreplay. The man's cock is hopeful, inquisitive. The woman's pubic pasture is a dew-drenched meadow.

JEAN-FRANCOIS: Oh my God.

ALPHONSINETTE: He asks her, "Now?" She says, "OK, my love," and reaches to her bedside table. *(Sprays.)* A few passes with Alphonsinette's invention and he is ready. She smiles invitingly. He says, "You spray well, my love. Not thickly like some. For example, Lucy Cormier sprays so much my dick feels like a hockey puck."

JEAN-FRANCOIS: Leave Lucy out of this.

ALPHONSINETTE: Sorry, I was trying to be funny. My couple has wild sex, no babies, no disease, no regret ... what do you think?

JEAN-FRANCOIS: Wow.

ALPHONSINETTE: The idea of the decade at least!

JEAN-FRANCOIS: It's not bad.

ALPHONSINETTE: Not bad! It's a sure thing! I'll be famous! I'm already practicing applications for when I go on the talk shows. *(Sprays randomly, carelessly.)* The slut. *(Sprays with prolonged industry.)* The fearful mother of six.

JEAN-FRANCOIS: Wait a minute! What happens after?

ALPHONSINETTE: After?

JEAN-FRANCOIS: How does he get rid of it?

ALPHONSINETTE: Rid of it?

JEAN-FRANCOIS: How do you remove a spray-on condom?

ALPHONSINETTE: Turpentine.

> *(JEAN-FRANCOIS yowls.)*

It's the only thing I've found that removes the rubber.

JEAN-FRANCOIS: You want him to roll over and stick his dick in a bowl of turpentine!

ALPHONSINETTE: It's a flaw, I admit it! We're working on solutions! We're going to hire a scientist who can figure something else. My poor Arvida man, he's all in favour of my invention. But I've made him test so many removers he's starting to lose the Big Jewel. And no one else will volunteer to try—

JEAN-FRANCOIS: Don't even ask.

ALPHONSINETTE: I would never endanger family.

JEAN-FRANCOIS: So what about those scientists? I'm told they cost money.

ALPHONSINETTE: Even a third-rate one can run you a hundred a day.

JEAN-FRANCOIS: Ahh.

ALPHONSINETTE: We don't need a lot! Just a little start-up capital. The government will kick in as soon as we've got a few thousand raised. And we know our MP. I've got a few things on him. We'll get students on summer grants. There's an agency that helps women without legs get started in business. It'll be clear sailing once we pitch our tents. We'll be rich. We can buy Arthabaska and throw out every last one of those bastards we're related to.

(Light can begin fading on ALPHONSINETTE.)

You can drive around Montréal in a car with black windows—it'll be like never leaving home. You'll get better, slowly. First the black windows, then a car with tint, then you can drive, maybe a convertible, maybe that Willys, then a bike. Before long we'll have you lecturing on TV. Speaking of the new entrepreneurial spirit sweeping the province. Jean-Francois this, Jean-Francois that. A name for the Nineties. Lights, cameras, celebrity ... Jean-Francois!

(Light is entirely off ALPHONSINETTE. Then light remains on JEAN-FRANCOIS, who is locked in an attitude of horror and wonderment, studying his thumb.)

Agoraphobia

(Light comes back up on AUNT ZÉNAÏDE, who is holding a bottle of pills.)

AUNT ZÉNAÏDE: You can't stay in here the rest of your life! As your senior relative, I forbid it!

JEAN-FRANCOIS: I'll go out when I'm ready.

AUNT ZÉNAÏDE: But when will that blessèd day be? The world isn't standing still!

JEAN-FRANCOIS: Let it move without me!

AUNT ZÉNAÏDE: Even Arthabaska's shaking a bit with the times. Now brighten up. Take some responsible measures.

JEAN-FRANCOIS: Maybe I'll pray.

AUNT ZÉNAÏDE: Screw that! Gobble these. *(Holds up bottle.)* Betablockers. *(When there's no response.)* JF! These babies top the 5BX and the Canada Food Guide by a country mile! In Arthabaska, we talk of nothing else. You want out? These will open the heaviest door!

JEAN-FRANCOIS: I'm not interested!

AUNT ZÉNAÏDE: Then you'll rot!

JEAN-FRANCOIS: I'll rot!

AUNT ZÉNAÏDE: Okay, rot. *(Shakes bottle, maybe pops a pill or two.)* Rot, see if your favourite aunt cares.

JEAN-FRANCOIS: I'm only interested in organic solutions.

AUNT ZÉNAÏDE: Fine, rot organically. *(Pause.)* So. Have you seen Alphonsinette?

JEAN-FRANCOIS: She comes around sometimes.

AUNT ZÉNAÏDE: She doesn't write me, you know.

JEAN-FRANCOIS: Forgive me, dear aunt, but why would she?

AUNT ZÉNAÏDE: She's my daughter! I want to know what she's doing with her life. At the very least she could send me a thank-you note.

JEAN-FRANCOIS: For bad-mouthing her?

AUNT ZÉNAÏDE: For investing.

JEAN-FRANCOIS: You put money into the spray!

AUNT ZÉNAÏDE: It's a cash cow! Xenon and I cleaned out the mattress for her. And for what? Sure, we have the satisfaction of seeing her on the talk shows. We can sit in our Arthabaska living room and bask in the reflection of her TV shadow. But when people ask, "What do you hear from that famous legless daughter of yours?" I have no answer because she doesn't write. No, Alphonsinette thinks I'm an ogre. That's her perception. An ogre.

JEAN-FRANCOIS: What do you see when you look at her?

AUNT ZÉNAÏDE: With my clear eye, I see my poor benighted limbless child, denying herself the purest solace there is: a good cry at the breast of her Maman. Instead she's down at Le Vagabond, consoling herself with every hard-up hard-on.

JEAN-FRANCOIS: If you stopped talking about her like that she might come back.

AUNT ZÉNAÏDE: But it's true!

JEAN-FRANCOIS: She's been with the same guy for years!

AUNT ZÉNAÏDE: That Arvida dolt! Hah! *(Pause.)* It's not so bad out there, JF, I swear it. There's a lot of energy on the street you can't get in a garage. It might help you with your writing. Tell me there aren't substantial drawbacks to this life of yours.

JEAN-FRANCOIS: I never see a woman in a dress.

AUNT ZÉNAÏDE: That's bad, yes.

JEAN-FRANCOIS: Madame Cormier only ever wears slacks.

AUNT ZÉNAÏDE: Even Xenon wouldn't look at that one. The daughter, yes, but—

JEAN-FRANCOIS: I can't see the river. I can't smell the deep water and you can't even see the mountain from my bedroom anymore, not since the expressway got built. I only catch the sunset when it reflects off the Cormiers' windows. Rainbows? The sun spangling the afternoon lake? *(Shrugs continentally.)*

AUNT ZÉNAÏDE: This regret makes me hopeful change may follow.

JEAN-FRANCOIS: Nah.

AUNT ZÉNAÏDE: Your ancient Auntie can hope, can't she?

JEAN-FRANCOIS: Once, not long before this started, I went with Lucy Cormier to the beach. We were still lovers then and it should've been a good afternoon. You couldn't actually swim in the water—there were signs posted. But you could lie on real sand in the company of thousands.

AUNT ZÉNAÏDE: That's nice, eh? Real sand, the river—

(AUNT ZÉNAÏDE can be leaving.)

JEAN-FRANCOIS: I walked along the edge of the water, taking care to not let any part of me come in contact with it. I paced off a yard and did a census of what I could make out through the murk: one natural yoghurt cup, no preservatives; one bellied-up perch; a green garbage bag waving through the water like a giant manta ray. There was a thermal inversion that day, too. The air was foul; it'd been locked over Montréal for a week. Some said it came direct from Pittsburgh.

AUNT ZÉNAÏDE: Pittsburgh!

JEAN-FRANCOIS: I knew you'd appreciate that. Oh, and that day? There were three murders and six bank hold-ups, and on the bus home we saw someone dead on the road with the ambulance right there. It turned out the person had actually been killed by the ambulance as it was speeding somewhere else. And you tell me I should be getting out? You want me out in that? Here, there's the honest smell of warm dirt, the healthy sound of the cicadas outside, buzzing above the accessing traffic. Bits of sun slip through the walls there, and there, wherever the boards are splitting. Paint brushes line up like old soldiers ... my hub-caps are here, and philosophy, meditation, art.... *(Gestures out.)* Chaos. Fools. Disease.

Pessimism

(Introducing FATHER ROCKY.)

FATHER ROCKY: Even I don't say it's that bad!

JEAN-FRANCOIS: Father Rocky!

FATHER ROCKY: Why're you surprised?

JEAN-FRANCOIS: Sophie was so cruel to you at the hospital—

FATHER ROCKY: She was in pain. That anger—she didn't mean it for me. She's gone now; my duties lie with the living.

JEAN-FRANCOIS: What a lot of bullshit that is.

FATHER ROCKY: You may not know it, but you need me.

JEAN-FRANCOIS: Like I need the clap.

FATHER ROCKY: This defensive posture you adopt when confronted by the clergy—it hints of a torn heart.

JEAN-FRANCOIS: Oh Christ.

FATHER ROCKY: A heart insecurely secular.

JEAN-FRANCOIS: I'm not interested.

FATHER ROCKY: Your sister abused me with conviction, but you protest too much.

JEAN-FRANCOIS: Did Aunt Zénaïde send you?

FATHER ROCKY: God sent me.

JEAN-FRANCOIS: Did He get a phone call from my aunt?

FATHER ROCKY: She's worried. You're not answering your phone. She thought maybe you'd hung yourself from grief. She called me a dolt and in the next minute she begged me to look in on you. It's so typically ambivalent.

JEAN-FRANCOIS: We were the first generation to give up on the church, Sophie and me. After a thousand years of kissing the bum of every passing priest we who said, "That's enough, we go it alone from here on in." And we said it on behalf of all our ancestors. We purged the church right off the tree. The skin of faith slipped away so easily, like a lizard shedding—

FATHER ROCKY: Smoke?

(FATHER ROCKY pulls out a pack of Luckies; offers.)

JEAN-FRANCOIS: Just one. Then you have to go.

(FATHER ROCKY and JEAN-FRANCOIS light cigarettes; begin smoking. JEAN-FRANCOIS will adopt RAYMOND LOEWY mannerisms.)

You do that like a peasant.

FATHER ROCKY: I am a peasant.

JEAN-FRANCOIS: Don't sound so proud of it. Hold it like this. Turn your right foot out. Pose. And don't look so greedy when you inhale.

FATHER ROCKY: I've lost many sheep over the years, but the loss of you and your sister has hurt me the most. Of all the sheep in my fold, you and Sophie had the greatest potential for clutching God to your breasts.

JEAN-FRANCOIS: Wait a sec—did I say I'd given up on God?

FATHER ROCKY: Oh?

JEAN-FRANCOIS: I haven't given up on God, just on your bullshit.

FATHER ROCKY: "Theory without practice is barren."

JEAN-FRANCOIS: Yes, and we know who said that, eh?

FATHER ROCKY: My Lord and Saviour.

JEAN-FRANCOIS: Karl Marx!

FATHER ROCKY: Jesus Christ!

(They shrug.)

JEAN-FRANCOIS: Anyway, you're a fine one to talk about theory and practice.

FATHER ROCKY: Hold on! I've established a boxing club for young girls! And the province has given us permission to ladle soup every Thursday. They give us a schedule of acceptable soups and we spoon it out to the humble masses. Plus, I'm setting up a workshop for the handicapped in the church basement—we'll be threading rosary beads and mailing them to the faithful in Third World countries.

JEAN-FRANCOIS: Those aren't good enough reasons for me to show up at mass. And don't try frightening me into coming, either.

FATHER ROCKY: Then I appeal to your sense of compassion.

JEAN-FRANCOIS: Oh please.

FATHER ROCKY: The little boxing girls don't believe. They laugh at me. The bums who slurp my soup are too far gone to care; they've witnessed so much of the roughness of life. I'm even losing my grip on the handicapped. Your cousin Alphonsinette ridicules me at every turn. Her billboards surround my church. Evening mass is ruined by the flashing of her condom ads. If fear and practicality can't draw you back—can pity?

JEAN-FRANCOIS: I'm agoraphobic.

FATHER ROCKY: You can sit in the confessional.

JEAN-FRANCOIS: Sophie'd kill me.

FATHER ROCKY: Sophie's dead.

JEAN-FRANCOIS: She'd resurrect just to kill me.

FATHER ROCKY: Resurrection's been done.

JEAN-FRANCOIS: I don't believe in God.

FATHER ROCKY: You just said you did.

JEAN-FRANCOIS: I lost it.

FATHER ROCKY: Just like that.

JEAN-FRANCOIS: Sorry. I'll give you money for your soup kitchen.

(He begins footwriting a cheque.)

FATHER ROCKY: No one can say I didn't try.

JEAN-FRANCOIS: And I'll ask Alph to lay off the billboards.

FATHER ROCKY: I almost had you.

JEAN-FRANCOIS: I'm vulnerable right now. It would've been a false victory.

FATHER ROCKY: God doesn't care about methods! For him it would've been as noble a triumph as if I ... as if I'd brought your cousin Terry back to the straight and narrow path.

JEAN-FRANCOIS: Speaking of paths ...

FATHER ROCKY: What?

JEAN-FRANCOIS: Father, what is it you do in the gully?

FATHER ROCKY: It's not a gully anymore. It's an underneath-the-access-ramp.

JEAN-FRANCOIS: What do you do down there? It seems odd to look out my kitchen window and see a priest slipping down the gully path. And Madame Cormier says you go every day. Collecting hub-caps, are we?

FATHER ROCKY: I have a hobby.

JEAN-FRANCOIS: I can imagine.

FATHER ROCKY: I count dead birds.

JEAN-FRANCOIS: You count dead birds.

FATHER ROCKY: I count dead birds. I give them last rites. I bury them.

JEAN-FRANCOIS: You don't expect me to believe that—

FATHER ROCKY: Two years ago I was sweeping the front steps of the church and a rock dove fell at my feet. Overlooking the obvious symbolism of the act, a small bell rang in my head: hobby. After all, if God can see the little sparrow fall, the least I can do is keep a list. I wrote down "dove" and then it occurred to me that, as a priest, I had to do more than just look. So I buried. There's plenty of people keeping track of the live birds—I'll watch over the dead ones. And there's a great diversity of them in that bastardized gully—redstarts, thrushes, thrashers—

JEAN-FRANCOIS: You bury birds.

FATHER ROCKY: Yes.

JEAN-FRANCOIS: That's pathetic.

FATHER ROCKY: Is it any more so than burying your sister? And your parents? The Swappers. We all look for meaning in this life and, yes, tending to dead flying creatures is a nearly meaningless act. But if you add it all up, if you add up the number of nearly meaningless acts I've performed over the past two years, something develops. At least for me. And it's not for you to belittle that. It certainly isn't for you to define what has or hasn't meaning. Theory without practice? You're as rusty as that old Willys there. You cynics make me sick.

Love

(FATHER ROCKY can tear off his garment in disgust. Under-neath, he is LUCY CORMIER, JEAN-FRANCOIS' old flame. She might be wearing black—in mourning for SOPHIE.)

LUCY CORMIER: But there's no mountain in Toronto. A lot of won-derful gullies but no mountain. Your eyes are never pulled upwards there, just down. Not that I'll have eyes left to see anything with. I'm losing them to the computer screen.

JEAN-FRANCOIS: Sophie and I never computerized.

LUCY CORMIER: It's too bad. Your sister would have found it liberat-ing. She could've written less, more quickly. Anyway, my eyes and my back are going, my ovaries are vapourized. I never realized how truly mundane life could be until I transferred there. Toronto is a city vindicated by the VCR. The only relief from boredom is fear. There's a vast parking garage under my building—it terrifies me. When I go down to my car I whistle a tune, not to sound bold, but because I figure there's a one-in-a-million chance I'll be whistling the song that's special to my killer. Maybe the song his mother whistled to him at the breast. So he'll spare me. My apartment's a boring box, my job's tedious; all I have is the terror in between.

JEAN-FRANCOIS: We'd go down to the gully. This is the same gully the expressway molested but in those days it was deep, deep enough to save the coolness of the night all day long, and dense enough to grant us the privacy to explore each other's body ... far away from the vigilance of the street.

LUCY CORMIER: Remember how our folks watched us?

JEAN-FRANCOIS: They were afraid of what we were feeling. We had signals. Lucy'd be looking out her bedroom window and her mother would be scanning our house from downstairs, so I'd twitch my curtain.... Lucy'd see.... You'd see and down you flew, me too, we'd build such a head of steam—

LUCY CORMIER: It was magic—

JEAN-FRANCOIS: Yeah, there was magic in this ugly cul-de-sac—

LUCY CORMIER: The best part was, it was forbidden.

JEAN-FRANCOIS: It drove them crazy. And we'd lie in the dirt, we'd fuck our way through that gully, from one bank to the other—

LUCY CORMIER: On the culvert—

JEAN-FRANCOIS: Beside the culvert—

LUCY CORMIER: In the dirt, against the tree, straddling the log—

JEAN-FRANCOIS: And when we were done we'd rinse ourselves in our spit and I'd brush you dry with the flat leaves.... We'd lie there for hours, just off the path....

LUCY CORMIER: Ahead of me, inches from my face, there were those thin pools of sunlight marking the path, and Maman's cat would creep along and stare at us.

JEAN-FRANCOIS: Up on the street the car doors would thunk, but the sounds you and I made stayed a secret down there.

LUCY CORMIER: Look what I've got. *(Pulls out a bottle of condom spray, gives a sample spray or two.)* I remembered our little rubber cemetery—remember how you'd mark each little burial with a twig? You've always been so careful about unforeseen tragedy.

   (JEAN-FRANCOIS is kissing LUCY CORMIER; she kisses him.)
   JF?

JEAN-FRANCOIS: Mmm.

LUCY CORMIER: Let's go.

JEAN-FRANCOIS: Go? Go where?

LUCY CORMIER: The gully. I've thought of nothing else. The whole drive down. All through your sister's mass. Let's go.

JEAN-FRANCOIS: Out?

LUCY CORMIER: Yes! We're in here—and the gully's out there.

   (JEAN-FRANCOIS is demurring.)

   It's the same gully, JF, I'm the same Lucy, it's the same sunlight, same path—

JEAN-FRANCOIS: I can't!

LUCY CORMIER: And the dirt, the sunlight—

JEAN-FRANCOIS: I can't go—

LUCY CORMIER: The broad flat leaves, the sunpools, me, you—

JEAN-FRANCOIS: No!

LUCY CORMIER: Yes!

JEAN-FRANCOIS: *(Pushing LUCY CORMIER away.)* I can't go out!

LUCY CORMIER: Yes you can!

JEAN-FRANCOIS: I'm agoraphobic! You don't understand! I physically cannot step out. I'd choke. I'd stop breathing. I couldn't breathe—

LUCY CORMIER: I don't buy this agoraphobic shit.

JEAN-FRANCOIS: It's true!

LUCY CORMIER: Really? That's not what I think. That's not what anyone thinks. Agoraphobia? *(Sound of disgust.)*

JEAN-FRANCOIS: I have a disability certificate—

LUCY CORMIER: I'm supposed to be impressed by that? I'm supposed to believe a piece of paper you got some quack to sign? Why don't you just admit it! If you wanted to go out, you would—but you don't want to. And the reason you don't want to is—you're scared.

(JEAN-FRANCOIS turns away.)

You're spineless. You're too fucking spineless to even bury your sister. You're even afraid of me! Admit it! You're afraid of me!

JEAN-FRANCOIS: Maybe I don't want you.

LUCY CORMIER: Oh, you want me all right. You want me, you want it nice and easy and safe, with no risk, no terror. You want it all your own way, but that's not how it works. So fine, stay here, but remember what you're missing.

(Smashes at hub-caps.)

You have these and this stupid car and your stupid writing but you don't have me.

(Just about to exit.)

I've never loved anyone like I love you. When you bunkered down here I couldn't bear the thought of never seeing you again, of never being with you, never being—in your arms or.... I moved away. It was the only thing I could do. But this time, it's different. This time I'm going voluntarily. Toronto isn't my first choice of places to be but it has one important advantage over here—it doesn't have you.

(LUCY CORMIER exits.)

JEAN-FRANCOIS: Wait! Wait!

(JEAN-FRANCOIS might run to the garage window. He might try and leave, but fail. Finally he collapses under the weight of his loss, and begins to grieve for his sister.)

Sophie. Sophie. Oh Sophie. *(etc.)*

A Bit of a Relapse, Then a Start to Recovery

(SOPHIE appears with a sheet, scissors and mirror. She'll wrap JEAN-FRANCOIS and start to snip at his hair.)

SOPHIE: *(Wrapping him.)* Why don't you just let it grow long like Jesus?

JEAN-FRANCOIS: It would give Father Rocky hope.

SOPHIE: But nobody's going to see you in here.

JEAN-FRANCOIS: Personal design transcends interiors.

SOPHIE: That's smart. You think it up?

JEAN-FRANCOIS: It's from Loewy.

SOPHIE: *(Wielding scissors.)* I might have guessed. So what's the personal design in coiffure this month? How about a brush-cut!

JEAN-FRANCOIS: Eggheads don't look good brush-cut.

SOPHIE: You're not an egghead. You're a garage populist.

JEAN-FRANCOIS: Well, I just want a trim. And nothing off the front. Any mail?

SOPHIE: No.

JEAN-FRANCOIS: Are we of no consequence to the mailers of mail?

SOPHIE: Apparently.

(Letter falls out of SOPHIE's pocket to floor.)

JEAN-FRANCOIS: But, what's that?

(SOPHIE stands on it.)

That's a letter. Who's it from?

SOPHIE: *(Picking it up.)* No one.

(JEAN-FRANCOIS grabs it.)

JEAN-FRANCOIS: *(Sniffs.)* I can smell Old Spice. It's from Cousin Terry.

> *(SOPHIE grabs it back.)*

Open it up!

SOPHIE: I already did. It was addressed to me.

JEAN-FRANCOIS: So read it!

SOPHIE: It's personal.

JEAN-FRANCOIS: *(Pouts.)* This is nice. The garage begins to have secrets. His sister begins concealing things from him. Is it for his own good? I think not. Information withheld never benefits anyone. *(Sighs.)* "The way of the egghead is hard."

SOPHIE: Oh for God's sake, it's just a letter. He smashed his car.

JEAN-FRANCOIS: The Nash! And you weren't going to tell me!

SOPHIE: Of course I was going to tell you. He was driving down the Hollywood freeway and a man jumped in front of him and he rolled it.

JEAN-FRANCOIS: Terry tells things so much more poetically.

SOPHIE: Jesus Christ. *(Picks up letter, reads manfully.)* "I'm minding my own beeswax when this man leaps in front of my tiny auto and bounds across the umpteen lanes and into the bushes on the far side. Now Sophie, do you know, I've caught all this action in my head-lights and I tell you the man was like a scared deer. Bambi-esque. I was just so startled I lost all control and consequently the perky Nash was ditched."

JEAN-FRANCOIS: Is Terry OK?

SOPHIE: He's fine but listen to this. "And do you know, as God is my Big Witness, you'll never guess who the man was leaping in front of me."

JEAN-FRANCOIS: Who?

SOPHIE: "Jean Lesage."

JEAN-FRANCOIS: Jean Lesage. That's the stupidest thing I've ever heard.

SOPHIE: It gets worse. In the next paragraph he says Lesage not only bounded across the freeway, I'm quoting, *(Reading.)* "He leapt into my waiting soul. I am the reincarnation of Jean Lesage." Terry Terry Terry—

JEAN-FRANCOIS: *(With her.)* —Terry Terry. There's no possible way, you know. He must have been fifteen at least when Lesage died.

SOPHIE: He admits the reincarnation isn't quite taking.

JEAN-FRANCOIS: *(Shakes head.)* Too many years and too much dirty linen, I'd say. But shit, all this Lesage stuff; Terry's got to find his own heroes. He can't always be stealing ours. Next it'll be Raymond Loewy and then it'll be Adlai Stevenson. And Terry doesn't even know the first thing about populism.

SOPHIE: He sleeps with everybody.

JEAN-FRANCOIS: It's not the same thing. *(As SOPHIE snips.)* Careful of the sides. *(Pause.)* What else did he say?

SOPHIE: Hollywood's going downhill. He says it used to be enough if a man looked good in a swimming pool but now everyone's got balance sheets shoved up their alleghenies. It's rough on him. When he first arrived he was so popular.

JEAN-FRANCOIS: In certain circles.

SOPHIE: And now he's reincarnating on the Hollywood freeway.

JEAN-FRANCOIS: As Aunt Zénaïde says, "Nothing you can do about genetics." Anything else?

SOPHIE: *(Pause.)* He wants me to visit.

JEAN-FRANCOIS: *(Pause.)* I know.

SOPHIE: How do you know?

JEAN-FRANCOIS: I read the letter.

SOPHIE: It was addressed to me!

JEAN-FRANCOIS: You shouldn't've left it out.

SOPHIE: Christ, Jean-Francois, it was personal!

JEAN-FRANCOIS: He's a real bastard for trying to lure you out there.

SOPHIE: It's only a visit! He needs a car! That Willys is just gathering dust. I'll drive it out.

JEAN-FRANCOIS: You'll get mugged by a hitchhiker in Iowa and your corpse will be cut up into little pieces and—

SOPHIE: I'm taking Lucy Cormier for company. She's studying self-defence. I'm picking her up in Toronto and we're heading west.

JEAN-FRANCOIS: What if the car breaks down? Where are you going to find spare parts for a 1955 Willys Aero Ace?

SOPHIE: You worry too much.

JEAN-FRANCOIS: You really think you'll like it out there? It's awful in L.A. Even Terry says that. You'll have a huge let-down. You'll be depressed for months. You'll get all the way to the coast—barring a bloody encounter with a serial killer—you'll get out there and you'll end up like Terry: disillusioned, colour-enhanced, dried-up, used-up, a crumpled Dixie cup tossed on the side of the Hollywood freeway.

SOPHIE: And all this in two weeks.

JEAN-FRANCOIS: *(Pause.)* You won't come back.

SOPHIE: Of course I will.

JEAN-FRANCOIS: Terry didn't.

SOPHIE: Terry had no choice. And he didn't have anyone to come back to. I've got someone who needs me. One way or another, I'll never leave you.

> *(SOPHIE has finished cutting. She hands JEAN-FRANCOIS the mirror and puts down the scissors.)*

How's that?

JEAN-FRANCOIS: Very nice. A bit post-modern—

> *(SOPHIE swats him.)*

—but very nice.

SOPHIE: I should start a salon, eh?

JEAN-FRANCOIS: You could learn to cut hair with your feet.

> *(SOPHIE is moving off and laughing.)*

You'd make more money than Alphonsinette.

> *(SOPHIE has reached the door. JEAN-FRANCOIS is finding grey hairs. For the first part of the following speech he'll also be trying to cut his own hair, holding the mirror etc., and it is an awkward process.)*

Oh oh. What's this? A prominent grise! *(Pulls it.)* Ow. *(Pulls others.)* Yow! Yee-ow! She didn't visit Terry. I kept after her day and night and when it looked like I wasn't getting anywhere I moved some crucial parts from the Willys and mailed them off to Pittsburgh. To Terry's old address. To the city that welcomed him with smoky arms. Where he built up his muscles and girded his loins for the attack on Hollywood. Where he would flex and ungird, and see the dead father of the Quiet Revolution bounding in front of his Nashlights. Where he could be visited by ghosts, but not by Sophie. Because she was here with me. Because I made her stay here....

(SOPHIE is on the phone to him.)

SOPHIE: You'll have to leave the garage.

JEAN-FRANCOIS: No.

SOPHIE: You can only sustain illusion for so long, then rot sets in.

JEAN-FRANCOIS: I'm not rotting.

SOPHIE: With time, fantasy loses its beauty and becomes just another foolish affectation.

JEAN-FRANCOIS: What do you know about fantasy?

SOPHIE: I know what it isn't. What I'm feeling—is not fantasy.

JEAN-FRANCOIS: *(Whispering.)* I'm sorry, Sophie.

SOPHIE: I'm not coming home.

JEAN-FRANCOIS: There are ways.

SOPHIE: No.

JEAN-FRANCOIS: Yes!

SOPHIE: You'll quickly lose your power to imagine me back.

JEAN-FRANCOIS: Don't say that!

SOPHIE: I have to.

JEAN-FRANCOIS: *(Pause.)* Does it hurt so much?

SOPHIE: Forget about me. Physical pain I can deal with. JF—listen to me! You're going to become ugly in there. Isolation—it breeds stupidity. You'll become ugly and cross with the world. March to the sea! Promise me you'll do that! JF! Oh, JF!

(And now JEAN-FRANCOIS begins to write a short poem with his feet. He begins in torment, but quickly he becomes calm.)

Farewells

(This scene includes ALPHONSINETTE, RAYMOND LOEWY, AUNT ZENAÏDE and JEAN-FRANCOIS. It starts with ALPHONSINETTE roaring on stage, heavily into the Mexican motif; sombrero, castanets etc. JEAN-FRANCOIS snaps to.)

JEAN-FRANCOIS: Oh God.

ALPHONSINETTE: Careem-ba! Juan-Francisco, Juan-Francisco! I've come to say "Adios amigo!"

JEAN-FRANCOIS: Where ever are you going?

ALPHONSINETTE: Acapulco—Mé-hee-co. I'm moving the whole she-bang down there.

JEAN-FRANCOIS: Why?

ALPHONSINETTE: Cheap labour, for starters. And the Ministry of Health is on my ass.

JEAN-FRANCOIS: Didn't you fix the turpentine thing?

ALPHONSINETTE: Yeah, we got that solved all right.

JEAN-FRANCOIS: With?

ALPHONSINETTE: Diet Pepsi.

JEAN-FRANCOIS: That's an advance?

ALPHONSINETTE: Marginally. Trouble is, prolonged use of Diet Pepsi can eat away the penis, so the Feds are whipping my baby off the market. There's hypocrisy for you! The Pill causes strokes and God knows what else, but all I do is scald a few wieners and they shut me down.

JEAN-FRANCOIS: It seems funny, doesn't it, making millions preventing thousands, then having to move to a more benign climate. And all because a train took off your legs. It's the old amputation-opportunity thing.

(ALPHONSINETTE laughs and pulls JEAN-FRANCOIS down for a hug. Tender.)

We'll see each other again.

ALPHONSINETTE: I doubt it. There'll be great reluctance in certain quarters to letting me back in the country.

JEAN-FRANCOIS: Maybe I'll come to Mexico.

ALPHONSINETTE: Whoa! Can this be my JF talking?

JEAN-FRANCOIS: You're all the family I have left. I don't count your Maman and Xenon or any of the other Arthabaskan clods. You're the entrepreneurial hope of the clan. And, terrifying though it might seem, I'm the intellect.

ALPHONSINETTE: Doesn't scare me. And there's a lot of hills in Acapulco, it's true. I'm going to need someone to push me around.

JEAN-FRANCOIS: What about your tester from Arvida?

ALPHONSINETTE: He doesn't walk too good anymore. *(Hands over condom sprays.)* Here. Factory seconds, use 'em in good health. *(Siren in distance.)* Oh oh. Time for Alphonsinette to exit. I've got Arvida idling on the access ramp. *(Kisses JEAN-FRANCOIS.)* If anyone asks, tell them I ran off to Pittsburgh—there's a family precedent, eh?

JEAN-FRANCOIS: Yeah—I'll be seeing you. Before you know it, maybe.

(ALPHONSINETTE turns around. She's become RAYMOND LOEWY. He picks up the condom spray.)

RAYMOND LOEWY: *(Reading.)* Le Vagabond Pharmaceuticals?

JEAN-FRANCOIS: My cousin owns the company.

RAYMOND LOEWY: She needs a designer.

JEAN-FRANCOIS: She was getting her bottles from a mouth-spray company.

RAYMOND LOEWY: Every object has its ideal form.

JEAN-FRANCOIS: But a condom spray?

RAYMOND LOEWY: Think.

JEAN-FRANCOIS: I suppose it could glow in the dark, so you can find it on your bedside table.

RAYMOND LOEWY: Good.

JEAN-FRANCOIS: And it could have a flashlight attached, so you could aim?

RAYMOND LOEWY: Excellent. *(Pulls out Luckies.)* You want another of these?

JEAN-FRANCOIS: Sure.

(RAYMOND LOEWY and JEAN-FRANCOIS smoke in great style.)

RAYMOND LOEWY: The great regret of my life is I didn't invent Tupperware.

JEAN-FRANCOIS: Now that's ideal form. Especially the jello moulds.

RAYMOND LOEWY: A few thoughts. Your sister was right. Simplicity is the goal. That's not the same as all that "less is more" nonsense—don't get the two confused. Reduction enhances. Form should be humble. I had to inhale the art of a thousand years before I could design my Coke bottle. But JF? I'm just a designer. I'm the best designer to have ever walked this planet—but that still isn't reason enough to make a cult of me.

JEAN-FRANCOIS: —Mr. Loewy.

RAYMOND LOEWY: Raymond.

JEAN-FRANCOIS: What would I lose by leaving here?

RAYMON LOEWY: Nothing. Not a thing. Not as long as you honour the essence of who you are and carry it into the future. After all, if you forget who you are, how can you understand what you might become?

(Car honk.)

(Continental shrug; turns to leave.) By the way. On the drive up, in central Vermont, we were passing through a rock cut and someone had spray-painted "God/Agog".

JEAN-FRANCOIS: That's from my sister.

RAYMOND LOEWY: I know.

JEAN-FRANCOIS: Raymond!

RAYMOND LOEWY: *(Half-turning.)* Mm?

JEAN-FRANCOIS: I'm going to tape a foot-something in the Lever Building!

(RAYMOND LOEWY smiles and waves continentally; he makes a full turn; he is now AUNT ZÉNAÏDE.)

AUNT ZÉNAÏDE: I see Alphonsinette the slut's been here. *(Picks up condom bottle.)* You know she's wanted for fraud, heh? That spray-on rubber—it never worked. She sold a million bottles and nine months later the stinking birth rate's shot up higher than Duplessis' fondest dream. They're saying she's given an entire culture a generation's reprieve. Her idiot parents are going to starve in Arthabaska, but she's saved a culture. So look: are you still feetwriting?

JEAN-FRANCOIS: Trying.

AUNT ZÉNAÏDE: Just because your sister's gone, doesn't mean you should stop. How come you say "trying"?

JEAN-FRANCOIS: People won't leave me alone.

AUNT ZÉNAÏDE: Is that a hint? Fine, hints I take for free. I'm only here out of respect for your father's memory. Just stick my head in the foot-garage and then haul my ass back to Arthabaska. Xenon's not well. Now that I've got the upper hand he's feeling the back of it. It's been forty-five years and finally, now, when I get the urge, I deck him. I've discovered there's an element of truth in violence. I've learned the secret men know from birth. I'm empowered!

(AUNT ZÉNAÏDE is shaking her fist at JEAN-FRANCOIS.)

So watch what you write about your old aunt!

(AUNT ZÉNAÏDE continues to shake her fist at JEAN-FRANCOIS, but he catches her arm and kisses her hand.)

(Fondly.) You men. You don't fool me. *(Gently; pulls him to her.)* Write us some modern truths, boy. Get those toes in motion. Do something. Do something—

JEAN-FRANCOIS: Or rot.

(AUNT ZÉNAÏDE releases JEAN-FRANCOIS and exits. JEAN-FRANCOIS watches her go. He remembers the phone conversation.)

(On phone.) Sophie? Sophie—are you still there?

A Decision Is Made

(With JEAN-FRANCOIS and SOPHIE.)

SOPHIE: Just let the front lawn grow over. It'll drive Madame Cormier nuts.

JEAN-FRANCOIS: I might get it paved.

SOPHIE: That's even better. Cement a hub-cap or two on it—really put her under. The roof's going to need repairs in six years. I've left the name of the company in a file on my dresser. And the furnace, too— you'll have to replace it by the end of the century. The Korean will deliver your food and his boy will go to the bank for you, at least until he's too busy with university. They promised.

JEAN-FRANCOIS: You're sounding like Aunt Zénaïde.

SOPHIE: I'm dying and you say that?

JEAN-FRANCOIS: I mean, the way she was giving me orders after Maman and Papa died.

SOPHIE: You could do worse than to get out her 5BX book. Lucy tells me you're looking a bit puffy.

JEAN-FRANCOIS: She hasn't seen me.

SOPHIE: Madame Cormier's got a telescope now. Listen, you should be nicer to her, and when Lucy comes to see you, be nice to her, too. And, if you can, make peace with Arthabaskans and try get Cousin Terry to come home. He's a mess.

JEAN-FRANCOIS: And Father Rocky?

SOPHIE: Don't let the church within a block of your life, ever again. You can contemplate God but don't you dare do it in the company of strangers. *(Pause.)* I could've wished you were here.

JEAN-FRANCOIS: Why are you saying that now?

SOPHIE: I don't know. Sorry. Everyone else says it and I guess I'm just repeating. Forget I mentioned it. But what if Aunt Zed drove you down here and parked in the lot beneath my window ... we could wave ... would that be so bad?

JEAN-FRANCOIS: The last thing she told me before she slipped into incoherence was that she was concentrating on a chip in the enamel of her sink.

SOPHIE: It's at head level. I'm taking the chip from the larger whole and by blocking out everything that surrounds it, I'm enhancing its beauty.

JEAN-FRANCOIS: I was afraid that the pain she was suffering, and the smells and the noise of the hospital would be too much for her, that they'd overwhelm her capacity to reduce, but no—

SOPHIE: The chip's as beautiful, as good as a berry on the Cormier hedge or the waxwing feather Father Rocky brought me from the gully ... or even the snub of Raymond Loewy's prize car....

   (Light off SOPHIE.)

JEAN-FRANCOIS: She was only eighty pounds when she died. She weighed seven at birth and I think she was trying to get back to that. Aunt Zénaïde looked after the burial. Sophie's in Notre-Dame-Des-Neiges, alongside my parents. Naturally, I had her cremated. And now I've just written my very first short piece. It's amazing being so reduced.

   (SOPHIE reappears. She's dead. JEAN-FRANCOIS hands her the poem.)

SOPHIE: *(Reads it.)* It's really good. It's beautiful. *(Counting.)* You've only used four words. Poor Lord Tennyson.

JEAN-FRANCOIS: He's flown the coop. And now I'll be writing these.

SOPHIE: And. *(Holds up poem.)*

JEAN-FRANCOIS: And.

SOPHIE: And? *(Smiles, holds out poem.)*

JEAN-FRANCOIS: *(Taking poem from SOPHIE.)* I'll have to do something with it.

   (Light off SOPHIE, who is able to go now.)

In the life of every nation there's a moment of hush, a twenty-minutes-to-the-hour pause when the collective will quietens. And then swells. It's as if we're all walking with linked arms into Lac Aylmer and, just before that cold water reaches our crotches, we stop.

And then, with a sigh that runs the length of our line, we settle into the lake, we immerse in the waters, right to our necks, together.

And in that moment there's sadness, an awareness of pain, an acknowledgement of change. And then an inkling of joy. Am I right?

(Announcing.) To the amazement of everyone on the cul-de-sac Birch, Jean-Francois, in the early evening of *[today's date]* flung open the door of his garage.

> *(Garage door is opening; colour outside. JEAN-FRANCOIS looks out, turns back.)*

There's one last leaf on my tree. It's coloured. All its brother and sister leaves have preceded it to the ground. Why is this last one hanging on? What made its stem so minutely stronger?

> *(JEAN-FRANCOIS looks again; turns back to audience again.)*

And in the second it takes us to marvel at its tenacity, there is a wind come up. The leaf flutters and protests. It leans back against a branch. As if resting. A new breeze flings it forward again. I can see that stubborn stem tear. The leaf unites with the open air.

This is the time.

This is the time.

This is the time.

> *(JEAN-FRANCOIS leaves.)*

> *(The End.)*